(143200)

Condition: F/VG+

Edition: 1st   Printing:

Size

Jacket: w/DJ   Pages: pp(INDEX)

Comments: 1/2" DJ tear near the (15) pu
Has a 2 page handwritten SDA letter in envelope
laid in.

Keywords: LB   Christmas, Christmas
Pageants, Christmas Poetry

Aurora

Price: 26⁰⁰

A CHRISTMAS MEDLEY

A CHRISTMAS MEDLEY

By

ELISABETH W. MORSS

BOSTON
BRANDEN PRESS
PUBLISHERS

*With affection and appreciation,
Part I is dedicated to Frances Dorwin Dugan,
Part II to Carl and Martha Bihldorff*

> Now do the great soft wings
> The captains touch and kings
> And for a moment fill
> The Earth with peace, goodwill.

PART I.

A Christmas Miscellany for Reading Aloud

What is Christmas?

It is a visual delight, catching our eyes with the bright displays in homes and shops and the rich colors of fruits and flowers, holding our eyes in the paintings and stained glass and candles.

It is a taste treat in the special foods of a holiday season, some for the one day only.

It is joy for the ears—bells and the music and the lift to a man's greeting. The carols live on for their own sweet charm as well as for Christmas Past.

It is a marvel for the nose. What is more festive, really, than the spicy smell of baking and the fragrance of the tree?

It is a sampler for touch, the ribbons and crisp papers, the party dress and gift scarf and tie, the best linen cloth and china and the prickly-soft tinsel and pine.

But above all and all these, it is a time for the heart, warming with memories, with today and tomorrow. It is passed along by so many hands in so many ways, and it rises up from inside us, from our inmost selves. Surely it comes with the possibility of love and the hope in a new small child.

To Sing for Christmas Eve, Beacon Hill, Boston

Handbells and carolling, joy on the Hill,
　　Christmas be Christmas, our
　　　　Dream of it still.
Families gathered and friends come to stay,
　　Christmas be reverent,
　　　　Christmas be gay!
Christmas be tree on a newly waxed floor,
　　Crêche on the table and
　　　　Wreath on the door.
Christmas be heartfelt, in big things and small,
　　Christmas be everywhere
　　　　Open to all.

[9]

Christmas be wonder for living and light,
    First for the stars, then the
        City tonight—
Handbells and carolling, joy on the Hill,
    Christmas be Christmas, our
        Wish for you still!

A Christmas Ballad

Dusty shoes on the white highway,
    Dusty shoes and the feet in them,
They have been travelling far today,
    Far on the road to Bethlehem.
A town, a camp, and a town again,
    The way is rough and hard—
Over a hill and down again
    And into a wide inn-yard.
In through the gate, a little faster,
    Steps that were growing slow—
Call for a boy to fetch the master
    Out from the warm hearth-glow.
"Master, a room, if you are able."
    "Sir, there is none to be had."
"Then I sleep with the beasts in the stable.
    Bring me a lantern, lad."
"It's useless, sir, to send for a light.
    The inn rooms overflow,
And I rented the stable for the night
    Many an hour ago."
Wearily, wearily turn the feet
    And pause at the stable door,
Feeling the hay so soft and sweet
    Spilled on the stable floor.
The guests before you are there inside,
    Shoes that are grey and worn,

A man from Galilee and his bride
    And a baby, newly born.
And shepherds lean on their crooks and pray
    And marvel to see the child.
Shoes, you and I will slip away,
    But see, how the mother smiled.
The highway gleams in the lonely night,
    Wind is a traveller's sigh,
One of the stars is very bright
    Low in the evening sky.
Dusty shoes, as you take your road,
    Dusty and worn and grey,
You never know what the great star showed.
    Dawn is Christmas Day.

Mary

She had to be there, for her time had come,
    Body taking over,
    Soul half-numb.

She had to be there, from the stable loft
    Pulling hay to make her
    Bedding soft.

She had to be there, and she wrapped the child,
    Anxious till she knew, and
    Then she smiled.

She had to be there, surely not alone.
    Kind hands must have helped her
    And her son.

A Carol

Lambs, come close, it's cold for him,
    He is sleeping, he is sleeping—
Warmth and comfort hold for him,
    Watch be keeping, watch be keeping—

[11]

Ox and ass, stay mute for him,
　　Dawn is breaking, dawn is breaking—
Shepherd, play a flute for him,
　　He is waking, he is waking.
　　　　Hearts and hopes belong to him,
　　　　Mary sings a song to him,
　　　　Christmas in the morning.

Manger, make a bed today,
　　Kindly sharing, kindly sharing—
Hay, a softness spread today,
　　Sweetly caring, sweetly caring—
Stable, give them rest today,
　　Till their going, till their going—
Bethlehem is blessed today,
　　Christmas knowing, Christmas knowing.
　　　　Hearts and hopes belong to him,
　　　　Mary sings a song to him,
　　　　Christmas in the morning.

The Three Kings

"I've lost the signs I marked before.
The night falls fast," said Melchior.
"The star begins to rise ahead—
Lift up your heart," Balthasar said.
And Caspar, riding after them,
Was miles beyond in Bethlehem.

"Who guides us to the stable door?
The town is dark," said Melchior.
"We follow where a star has led.
It leads us still," Balthasar said.
And Caspar listened, Caspar smiled,
For he already saw the child.

[12]

"Come, lay your gifts upon the floor,
And kneel to him," said Melchior.
"A manger makes a lovely bed—
Behold the King!" Balthasar said.
The star shone back from Caspar's eyes.
He knew he knelt in Paradise.

The Nights of Christmas

Sheep take fright from shepherds' fright.
Was it so on Christmas Night?
Had they huddled coldly there,
Sensing strangeness in the air?
When the lambs were crooked away,
Did they bleat and try to stay,
Carried starry hillsides down
To the darkness of the town?
  Joy would warm the flocks and men.
  It was Christmas even then.

When the precious gifts were put
At the manger's head and foot,
Where did Wise Men go to sleep,
With the shepherds and their sheep?
Or could room for them be made
As the tax was slowly paid?
In the stable still were three,
One the child they came to see.
  Love would shelter beast and man.
  That's how Christmas first began.

Mary's Songs

Long we journeyed, low and high,
To the little town,
Through the groves of olive trees,
Over green and brown.

Woeful were my weary feet,
Travel-stained my gown.
Star there was that Joseph watched,
And the days were flown.
Son of simple carpenter,
I would give thee crown.
Joseph gently picks thee up,
Gently lays thee down.

Now I lift thee high, so high
Thou canst see the town.
Grey-green are the olive trees,
And the earth is brown.
I shall set thee on thy feet.
Thou canst hold my gown.
Empty is the nest we watched—
All the birds have flown.
Thou hast played at carpenter
And a king to crown.
Gently do I pick thee up,
Gently lay thee down.

They have lifted thee so high,
Higher than the town,
There beyond the olive trees
On the barren brown.
Soldiers gambled at thy feet
For thy crumpled gown.
Till they pierced thy side we watched,
Till thy soul had flown.
Wood and thorn found carpenter—
I, too, wore thy crown—
Love now gently picks thee up,
Gently lays thee down.

[14]

Crèche

One Christmas, when St. Francis stayed
  In lonely hillside cavern,
An urgent message was relayed
  To every house and tavern.
Through field and fold and farmyard sent,
  It circled down the valley.
Across the village square it went
  And round the crowded alley.

He bade the people come to him
  And set a midnight timing,
And in the evening shadow dim,
  They gathered for their climbing.
They trembled leaving Greccio
  And sang a hymn to cheer them,
So dark the ways that few men know,
  So real the dangers near them.

Their lanterns wavered up the hill.
  They walked with worried glances.
They dreaded such a path, but still
  They trusted Brother Francis.
Soon all their forest fears had gone.
  A gladness filled their singing—
Above, monks' voices joined their own,
  Below, the bells were ringing.

And then what wonder met their eyes,
  What thrill of Christmas glory!
A stable was the saint's surprise,
  And how he told its story!
Some said that Christ himself came there,
  A baby in the manger,

While others felt the angels' care,
    No living thing a stranger.

Oh, happy night of Christmastide,
    Could we, too, hear the telling
And feel the same great peace inside,
    The love and joy upwelling.
Oh, little crêche whose figures fine
    My hands are now arranging,
Again we need the Christmas sign,
    For all the world is changing.

Postscript

One frosty New Year's morning,
    A stranger gave to me
A branch still green and tinselled
    From some old Christmas tree.
And when I would have spoken,
    "You think of it," said he.

At first I felt bewildered.
    I could not understand
This sudden gift of balsam
    Now in my mittened hand.
And then I saw the forest
    And sensed the hidden land.

I stood inside a clearing
    Where once a tree had grown.
The snow was melting strongly.
    I did not seem alone.
And on the ground before me,
    There lay a single cone.

[16]

A New England Christmas

Christmas was the children's day.
    Dad decreed a limit.
We were not to rise too soon,
    To enjoy, not skim it.
Mother checked a dozen lists,
    Card and gift and guest.
We helped Dad to trim the tree,
    This year's always best.
Grandma and the cook had planned
    Months ahead, I know—
From the oysters to the nuts,
    Everything just so.
Grandpa gave the family toast
    At the massive dinner.
(Grandma set her table well.
    No one could grow thinner.)
Now it's my turn for The Day.
    Envy in my look,
I reread the words I wrote—
    Grandma *and the cook!*

December

Month of the longest night,
Say that the sun is bright
And that a bird will bring
Song in its throat and Spring.

Month of the cold and storm,
Say that the sun is warm
And that a leaf will green
As it has always been.

Month when we seek a star,
Say it is not too far
And that the days increase
Into the light of Peace.

[17]

PART II.
A Pageant for Christmas

(Written for First Parish, Brookline, Massachusetts, and first performed there.)

For many years, Carl Bihldorff has been minister of First Parish, Brookline, an historically old gathering in its most recent building. The church has a happy tradition of a Christmas Eve evening carol service including the reading aloud of a story or poetry and a Christmas Sunday morning service which often presents a pageant. Long after I had graduated from being a lesser character in a pageant to a grown-up in a pew, my first surprise was that the Christmas services were not as happy for the minister as for the congregation. Carl lamented a dearth of new material for both services and the fact that the building, while visually suited for a pageant, acoustically makes it difficult for speaking parts. I began to think again of Christmas, the story, the personal message it had for me, the way Christmas has always brought together peoples across the world. My second surprise was to find myself writing these pages.

* * * *

General Stage Directions: Detailed directions are given in the Appendix. There are a prologue and three scenes without intermission. The scenery for Scene I and Scene III is a corridor of the Inn at Bethlehem; for Scene II, the stable of the Inn. The corridor shows an old, white-washed wall with a small opening for a window slightly to one side. Above, there should be a star which can be lighted and extinguished, and there are no furnishings. Music is part of the presentation.

CAST

a. Speaking characters:

FATHER, *who is the innkeeper*

MOTHER, *who is the innkeeper's wife*

OLDEST SON, YOUNGEST SON, DAUGHTER, *the innkeeper's three children*

[18]

NARRATOR

The children are close in age, the oldest about ten. Daughter is the youngest. Narrator should be an adult, a man whose voice carries well and with expression. (The minister of the church may take this role.) He stands out of the stage area, in a church, at the reading desk or in the pulpit, in a hall, by the main curtain.

b. Non-speaking characters:

An even number of ANGELS, who take charge of the scenery and stand as guardians of the stable in Scene II

   THE GRANDMOTHER
   THE HOLY FAMILY
   SHEPHERDS
   THREE WISE MEN
   PAGES TO THE WISE MEN, TOWNSPEOPLE and GUESTS AT THE INN

(Choir and musicians as desired)

PROLOGUE: *The introductory music or carol of an overture or a procession ends.* NARRATOR *speaks in a ringing voice.*

NARRATOR

Good people all, our play we bring—
The music sound, the carol sing!
The Christmas Story now begin,
A corridor at Bethlehem's Inn.
Mine host, his wife, and children see,
This night that shall so blesséd be.

SCENE I: *(Twilight, a corridor of the Inn at Bethlehem is revealed during brief music. Before the action starts, there is a slight pause for silence, perhaps introduced by a few very soft chords. Now the star shines.* FATHER *and* OLDEST SON *enter, followed by* MOTHER *and* DAUGHTER, *then* YOUNGEST SON. MOTHER *has* DAUGHTER'S *hand in hers. They are all simply dressed in earth-colors, their garments of rather coarse fabrics.* FATHER *carries a lantern. He stops midway and turns to speak to the others, who also stop.)*

[19]

FATHER (*handing the lantern to* MOTHER, *who drops* DAUGHTER's *hand to receive it*). Such a day. Such a day! I think I have never been so weary from running about and doing things in all my life. So many people wanting room and food, for themselves and for their animals! Everyone hungry and in a hurry and wanting something! At least, the inn is so full now I can't put up another person or another beast.

OLDEST SON (*going to the window and looking out*). There are more people coming, Father! I can see a man on the hill and a woman who is riding a donkey. The man's leading the donkey by a rope, and he's holding onto a thick staff.

FATHER. You'll have to meet them and tell them this inn is full and they can't stop here.

MOTHER (*nudging* OLDEST SON *from the window and looking out of it herself*). Oh, Father, you can't do that! It's late, and the man is old and the woman is great with child. They look so tired. There isn't another inn where they could go at this hour. Must you turn them away?

FATHER (*dubiously*). The only space I have left is a corner of the stable, if that would be of any use. I suppose they could sleep there— (*He hesitates and then goes off stage.* MOTHER *stays by the window, watching.*)

MOTHER (*to* OLDEST SON) Hurry and catch your father and ask him for some straw. If the travellers stay, it will make them more comfortable. (OLDEST SON *leaves.* MOTHER *again looks out of the window.*) Ah—they are staying! They're walking to the stable —the man is helping the woman to dismount from the donkey. (*To* YOUNGEST SON) They will need food, too, and a lantern. Here— (*she hands him the lantern she has been holding*) off with you! (*He goes out. She lifts* DAUGHTER *for a peek out of the window and sets her down again.* FATHER *enters.*)

FATHER. I guess they're cared for now. You were right, Mother—they are too tired to take another step. They're good people. They even thanked us, and it's little enough we can do for them.

[20]

MOTHER. Thanked us? They're the first guests to thank us in a long while! Who are they?

FATHER. The man is a carpenter from Galilee, and the woman is his young wife. They came here to be taxed, like most of our other guests tonight. The baby will be their first child.

OLDEST SON *(entering excitedly)*. Father! Mother! Joseph— I mean, Mary—I mean, the ones in the stable—the baby is coming! And did you see it? There's an awfully big star up in the sky!

MOTHER *(greatly surprised)*. A baby, and in our stable! *(Becoming efficient)* Quick! Run to the village and fetch your grandmother. She will know what to do. That's a good boy. *(She gestures with her hands, and OLDEST SON nods and hurries out.)* The poor thing, and so far from home. I'm sure she did not imagine that this might happen. *(She seems to think, then turns to DAUGHTER and lays a hand on the girl's shoulder.)* I've an errand for you, too, Daughter. In the carved chest, you'll find your swaddling clothes. I put them there, fresh and clean, when you had outgrown them. Please, will you bring them to me? I am going out to the stable. *(DAUGHTER nods and leaves.)*

FATHER. I'll go with you. I haven't given the donkey any water yet, and he must be thirsty. *(They go out. While music begins again to end Scene I and introduce Scene II, the angels appear and quietly change the setting.)*

SCENE II: *(Later the same night, the stable of the Inn. This scene is acted in pantomime. The only speaking part is that of NARRATOR, who will read the four poems alternately with music in smoothly flowing action. The angels now stand on each side of the stage area, evenly divided between right and left and outside of the stable. They are guardians, but not participants. They will remain in their positions until they change the scenery for Scene III and are dressed alike. If their hands are free, as they would be on a formal stage, some might hold holly and some palm branches. The star continues to shine. It is extinguished when the Holy Family departs. We see the stable and a colorful, traditional Nativity tableau. MARY and JOSEPH sit by the manger in which the baby lies. In back and to*

[21]

one side in an attentive group are the innkeeper and his family and the grandmother. They are joined by townspeople and guests who come and go with respectful curiosity and exchange comments with them. From the opposite side, SHEPHERDS, WISE MEN and PAGES will appear. When they leave, the last of the townspeople will leave, escorting the GRANDMOTHER. At the end of the scene, only the INNKEEPER and his family and the HOLY FAMILY are left on stage. The INNKEEPER and his family assist the HOLY FAMILY to depart and will wave good-bye to them. JOSEPH and MARY show their gratitude, and FATHER, who has had the lantern throughout Scene II, insists that Joseph take it. He does. With the innkeeper and his family alone and motionless and as if still watching their departing guests, the angels once more unobtrusively change the setting. After the star is extinguished, in making the scenery change the ANGELS retire.)

THE FOUR POEMS

The first will be read when just the HOLY FAMILY, the INN-KEEPER, and his family and the GRANDMOTHER are on stage. It should be read slowly and simply. The second poem is gay and informal, read as the first SHEPHERDS enter. The third comes between the departure of the last SHEPHERD and the arrival of the WISE MEN. It should be read with ceremony. The fourth poem should begin as the HOLY FAMILY actually leave and should be finished before the ANGELS change the scenery. It is to be read soberly but not somberly.)

1.

The little Jesu
    How softly he lay
There in the manger,
    Asleep in the hay.

The little Jesu
    How sweetly he smiled
There in the stable,
    The newly born child.

[22]

The little Jesu
How gently he moved
There with his mother,
Already so loved.   *(Music)*

2.

The shepherds came down from the hills in the night.
The villagers marvelled to see such a sight—
For how did they know they could leave all their sheep
Alone on the hillsides, so safely asleep?
They walked to the inn, and a pretty star shone
As if it were leading and urging them on.
They came to the stable with wonder and joy
And new little lambs for a new little boy.   *(Music)*

3.

Great are the Magi of the East
And wise as few are wise.
In palace towers the lonely hours
They chart the mystic skies.
Here they are striding,
Weary from riding,
Bearing the gifts of kings.

Great are the Magi of the East.
They hear a secret call—
It speaks to them of Bethlehem
And guides them to a stall.
Here they are striding,
Weary from riding,
Bearing the dreams of kings.

Great are the Magi of the East.
With incense, myrrh and gold
They journey on to hail the son
Whose birth a star foretold.

[23]

> Here they are striding,
>> Weary from riding,
>>> Bearing the love of kings.   *(Music)*

4.

This was a child of the humble folk,
>His birth-place least of all—
A bed of the straw for an ox and ass,
>The shelter of a stall.
Swiftly the news of his coming sped
>On watchful angels' wings.
First it was told to the shepherds there
>And after shepherds, kings.

From the beginning the humble folk
>Were quick to share the word.
Theirs were the hearts that had opened wide
>And theirs the ears that heard.
Person to person and small to great
>The joyful tidings wing—
First he is shepherd to all his flock,
>And after Shepherd, King.

Follow we, too, as the humble folk
>In peace, good-will to men.
Is there a star over Bethlehem?
>It shines today as then.
Let us uncover the joy again
>With love our angels' wings—
First be the shepherds to keep the trust
>And after shepherds, kings.

SCENE III: *(Very late on the same night, the corridor of the Inn at Bethlehem. The corridor is less well-lighted than in Scene I, the star has ceased shining and the music of the scenery-change fades softly into its last chords.* FATHER *enters, followed by the three children and, finally,* MOTHER. *All seem to be awaking from a beautiful dream.* FATHER *turns slowly to let the others come up to him, but* MOTHER *lingers by the window, looking out. They watch her.)*

FATHER *(slowly).* Well, they have gone now.

MOTHER. Yes. I can no longer see Joseph's lantern as they cross over the hill. They must be on the further side. *(She joins the others.)*

OLDEST SON. The star has gone, too. I shall always remember the star. It was so big and so bright, and it seemed to rise right above our Inn. One of the Wise Men said it did—he said it showed him the way here.

YOUNGEST SON. I shall always remember the Wise Men. They are kings, aren't they, Father? They looked like kings, and they had such fine camels. What will you remember, Mother?

MOTHER *(dreamily).* I shall remember the baby. I could never forget him. Wasn't he a sweet little boy? I've seen many children when they were just born, but somehow, he shines in my heart. *(More matter-of-factly)* I think the animals were very surprised to have a baby in their manger.

FATHER *(with a smile).* It was a funny bed for a baby, but I do believe he enjoyed it. *(To* DAUGHTER*)* What are you going to remember?

DAUGHTER. I shall always remember the gifts, the shepherds and their curly lambs and the gold and myrrh and frankincense. *(Shyly)* I liked the lambs best.

YOUNGEST SON. What are you remembering, Father? It's your turn to say.

FATHER *(tenderly).* I'm remembering my family and how we had a gift to give, too, though we didn't know it. *(Raising his arms and speaking with emphasis)* God bless them, and God bless us. We have been together. We were needed, and we are happy and at peace. It has been a wonderful, wonderful night.

[25]

(Smiling at them fondly, FATHER *lowers his arms to the shoulders of* YOUNGEST SON *and* DAUGHTER, *who have drawn close to him as he finished, one on each side. He leads them off stage with his arms still around them, and they go out slowly and happily.* MOTHER *takes* OLDEST SON'S *arm with a smile for him, and they go out behind the others. Standing on a signal from* NARRATOR, *choir and audience or congregation together sing a last carol. If the pageant has been in a church and it is desired to have them leave now, cast and choir will file out singing this carol also. As their procession starts, the angels can quickly make any adjustments to the scenery which the Director may wish. Then they will bring up the rear.)*

CURTAIN

All things and all things, they served at his birth,
Wood from the forest and ore from the earth,
Clay for the water-jar, wool for the thread,
Grain from the fields for the baking of bread.

All things and all things, they met at his side,
Ox for the ploughing and donkey to ride,
Neighbor and stranger with awe and delight—
Lamp-lit and star-lit, they came in the night.

All things and all things, they looked to this hour;
One was cathedral, another a flower.
Each was its meaning, a leaf on a tree,
Dream in fulfillment and hope still to be.

All things and all things, they quietly stay
While the world wanders the decades away.
Would it involve us? Our feet hesitate—
Is the door open for those coming late?

APPENDIX

STAGING THE PAGEANT

Because speaking has been kept to a minimum, it is all the more important that the lines be spoken distinctly and not mumbled or hurried. The timing throughout of all action and music should be smoothly managed. Any audience participation in the music should be limited to music before the Prologue and after the end of Scene III.

The way in which scenery and action are handled will depend upon whether the pageant is given on the stage of a hall or before the altar of a church. Perhaps a few suggestions may help—they are not instructions. On a stage, the wall might be an inner curtain with a window indicated upon it and a top valance. When the halves of this curtain are pulled back for the second scene, they should suggest a rectangular doorway with a lintel formed by the valance. The doorway should be wider than its height, and it lets us look into the stable in Scene II. In a church, there might be *a)* a fixed or movable framework or small stage with similar curtain and valance (no outer curtain as in a hall), or *b)* painted screens which can be pushed inward at an angle suggesting a front-view perspective of the side walls of the stable as one looks in, or *c)* a frieze of angels. There are no problems of setting up and changing the scenery in a hall with a formal stage, but there may be some in a church. Here, the scenery may be set up in advance or at the time by the angels. (It is moved by them as the action requires.) Stage wings in a church may be made of Christmas trees, or the choir placed so as to conceal the cast. For the latter, choir and cast might enter in procession, then divide to stand half to one side and half to the other. The cast would go beyond and behind the choir to be at least partially concealed. The angels should be evenly divided between right and left and members of the cast go to the side from which they will make their first entrance. The choir should not be where it interferes with the action. It is not part of the cast, and it might be preferable to locate it completely out of the stage area. When first staged by the church in Brookline, a single line of angels stood in one row to form the corridor wall, and dividing in the center, some stepped back at an angle to make the two side-walls of the stable. In poncho-type robes, arms linking them from shoulder to shoulder, they were a background frieze in robes of a soft monotone compatible with the impression they conveyed. In using this staging, one angel should hold a dark-colored frame suggesting a window in Scenes I and III. Another can hold a star mounted on a staff. When lighting or extinguishing the star is impractical, it can be raised and lowered or removed.

PROPERTIES: Scene I: A lantern. Scene II: The same lantern, shepherds' crooks, Joseph's staff, two or more lambs (which could be costumed children), Wise Men's gifts, manger with baby, seats of some sort for Mary and Joseph, and straw. Scene III: No properties.

MUSIC: All music, instrumental and/or choral, is at the Director's discretion. Each selection should cover the action for its time and be appropriate to it.

For a 20th Century "Bah! Humbug!"

Take a moment just to be
Underneath a living tree,
Looking upward where you are
To the twinkle of a star.

Take a moment just to know
How a smile begins to grow
And a happiness can shine
From the tinsel on a pine.

Take a moment just to say
"Christmas" in another way.
Watcher of the world tonight,
This is countdown for delight!

THE END